DESIGN: SOURCES AND RESOURCES

Following page:
A variety of letter forms in an irregular arrangement outside a French country store creates a decorative and eye-catching design. (Photograph: L. B. B.)

ICI GLACES MAISON

UNION EUROPÉENNE

éGe

La Slavia

BIERE DES GOURMETS

y'a bon...
BANANIA
LE PETIT DÉJEUNER FAMILIAL

Gillette

yon éGe
5% D'ÉCONOMIE

Granvillons Damer
GRAND VIN
..propre du monde !

DESIGN | SOURCES AND RESOURCES

LOUISE BOWEN BALLINGER · THOMAS F. VROMAN

 REINHOLD PUBLISHING CORPORATION / NEW YORK

TO   THELMA E. VROMAN   AND   RAYMOND A. BALLINGER

Designed by Thomas F. Vroman
Type Set by Graphic Arts Typographers, Inc.
Printed by New York Lithographing Corp.
Bound by Publishers Book Bindery, Inc.

CONTENTS

Introduction

This book is not intended to be a short cut to design nor does it try to set forth methods for the designer. His path must necessarily be one of slow, steady development since there is no royal road to art or design.

The authors hope to provide sources of inspiration and, by suggestion, inference, and synthesis, to lay the groundwork for greater understanding of the relationships in the arts of the past and the present and of their debt to the limitless world of nature.

In the following chapters a wide and visually stimulating cross-section of material drawn from nature and the past will be related to the principles of design. These relationships should be considered to be suggestive, not absolute, for it is the province of every artist to make his own syntheses and to draw his own conclusions so that his creative efforts will be unique expressions.

The word "design" is used to describe many things. It can mean the surface decoration found on a Pennsylvania German dower chest, the form of a soaring skyscraper, or the delicate structure of a suspension bridge. It can mean the print or pattern of a fabric, the composition of a painting, or it can be interpreted as the organization of a poem. The Greek word for design means poetry, so perhaps we could call design a combination of art and order.

Planned order surrounds us. A Beethoven concerto, a modern ballet, a bridge, a mural, the draperies in our homes, all reflect order and planning in some way. Of this we are probably aware. But what about the rhythmic movement of waves or the growth patterns of a tree? Nature is one of the richest sources for artistic inspiration and for examples of the principles of design. To the artist these examples do not represent a set of hard and fast rules to be followed blindly. He knows that the inspiration, the idea, not the principles, comes first. The art of the past is a treasure house of resource material drawn from nature and man's imagination, a reminder that man has been not only a creature of activity but a thoughtful, appreciative and perceptive artist.

In this era, bombarded as we are with the visual impact of books, magazines, posters, and television, there are too many who look but do not see. Today we need artists and educators who cultivate in themselves and others the habit of perceptive searching through which we learn to understand and value the disciplines of the visual arts.

CHAPTER 1 | NATURE AND THE HISTORIC PAST AS SOURCE AND RESOURCE MATERIAL

Man has always drawn information and aesthetic inspiration from nature. At first, his aesthetic response was wholly intuitive. Yet nowhere is the direct use of natural forms better expressed than in the superb animals painted on the walls of prehistoric caves.

As man emerged from the primitive state, he became consciously aware of form, color, movement and sound as creative forces. Art, as both an intuitive and conscious means of self-expression, developed. Civilized man began to interpret nature's forms, to adapt them to the material used and the area in which they were placed, sometimes realistically, sometimes highly stylized.

In the graceful interpretations of animal and plant life depicted on walls of Egyptian tombs, the essence of nature's design patterns has been captured for all time. Stylized forms of the lotus can be traced from Egyptian frescoes, through Greek painted ceramics, down to our own times. The mosaic floors and fresco wall paintings of the ancient villas of Rome and Pompeii brought indoors naturalistic interpretations of the plant, animal and aquatic life of the times. And at a time thought not to be overly concerned with the external forms of nature, we find details of plant and bird life accurately recorded on Medieval manuscripts while the whole was woven into elaborate designs to illuminate a letter or to form a carefully arranged border. Conventionalized forms of animal and plant life were used on the elaborately carved column heads of Romanesque churches in an effort to fit the form. In each of these examples, the natural form was adapted to a particular use but its intrinsic quality was not lost.

In contemporary times, the scope of nature's source material has been vastly extended. The eye has been aided by the camera, the microscope and the telescope. Details that had seemed unimportant parts of a whole have been revealed as exquisite and complete designs—starting points for creative imagination. The camera has helped us to see design possibilities such as those inherent in the pebbles on a beach, the many varieties of lichen, the textures of bark, geological formations, and undersea forms. Microscope and telescope have revealed completely new worlds: minute crystal forms, teeming organic life, the stresses of metal, the forms and colors of space.

Each new revelation continues to attest to the well-known dictum, "Order is nature's first law." But what is order? Is it merely machine-like duplication of form? Or is it nature's order—infinite in its variety and observable everywhere for those whose eyes not merely look but see? Order extends through all levels of nature, including human beings. We demand it in many areas of our lives, search for it in art, and learn its complexities from nature. Snowflakes all have a basic hexagonal structure yet no two are exactly alike. Each species of tree has its own characteristic structure, yet no two leaves on a branch are precisely identical. The waves of the sea break on the shore in unending rhythm, yet always with subtly varied intensities.

But how does today's designer apply the world's accumulated knowledge to his own work? Not by taking ideas intact from nature or from historic art forms, for such uncritical borrowing would only result in aesthetically empty work. He must use his resources in the light of the problem to be solved, the idea to be expressed, and the material to be used, for these are vital parts of any creative design. The process might be described as being "informed" by nature and is, like all creative processes, highly complex, not readily explained, and never the same. It includes conscious and unconscious thought, direct response to and stored memory of the thing studied.

The artist or designer who is truly alive and creative always finds interest in the subjects around him. But to be productive his interest must go beyond mere appreciation. He may observe, sketch, and study some aspect of insect life or plant structure merely for his own interest, with no immediate application in mind; but such studies become part of his resources and sooner or later, consciously or unconsciously, he will put this knowledge to practical use. Many designers find it valuable to make sketches of everything that interests them. A Leonardo da Vinci sketchbook, for instance, shows that the artist evolved some of his highly mechanical structures from his detailed study of grasses. Durer's block prints show obvious evidence of previous studies.

Designers use their eyes and hands at all times. Some use the camera as an extra means of recording resource material at hand, and most compile a wide variety of informative and inspirational material found in the better current publications. These might include illustrations, photographs, well-designed pages, and art from the past as well as the present. Such material gives the designer the opportunity to see how problems not unlike his own were solved by other artists. Forms and patterns he would not otherwise see—the structure of an atom, the beautiful use of marble veining and color in Renaissance buildings, the use of rhythm and line in ancient Greek pottery—may provide inspiration for solving his own design problem in a new and fresh way.

Awareness of nature and the past when combined with the designer's personal point of view and the demands of his own age are the basic ingredients for any work of art. But the designer must have more than appreciation of the past, sensitivity to order in nature, and knowledge of the accomplishments of his own time, more than understanding the principles of design and knowing how to apply them. He must also have that almost intangible quality that in its essence carries the stamp of individuality.

The poet Marianne Moore has said that "uniqueness is a by-product of sincerity." Yet the leaders of every era inevitably have followers who hope to become great through blind imitation, forgetting that the artists they imitate became great only through originality, honesty, and continual searching in an effort to solve problems and express ideas in ways peculiar to themselves. The unique and timeless quality of true creative expression, whether in a Medieval tapestry, a sensitive Japanese scene painting, or a Frank Lloyd Wright home, speaks eloquently of the designer's sincerity of idea and purpose.

The artist or designer must see, plan and try many solutions to a problem; he must study its require- ments, know its scope and limitations; he must analyze and evaluate as he works—rejecting or accepting his own ideas until a well-designed, unique work of art emerges. Only out of enthusiasm for an idea, nourished by the richness of knowledge, sincerity, and an individual point of view can a work of art be created. According to Harold Taylor, individuality comes from within. He puts it this way:

"But to achieve genuine individuality in the modern world one does not always try to be an individual. Individualism is achieved by trying to be honest with oneself, honest in one's judgments, tastes, and preferences; individualism is an outcome of this effort—it is not its purpose." [1]

This then, is the problem as well as the challenge for the artist and designer: to absorb and observe the limitless sources of the natural world, to enrich his own vision and understanding by the contributions of the past, and, in so doing, to move toward his own unique mode of expression that is of the spirit of his time.

[1] Harold Taylor, *Art and the Intellect*, New York: Museum of Modern Art, distributed by Doubleday and Company, Inc., Garden City, N.Y. 1960.

Cave Drawing from Altamira, Spain. An early example of man's observation of natural forms and his urge to express an idea graphically. (Courtesy: The Museum of Modern Art)

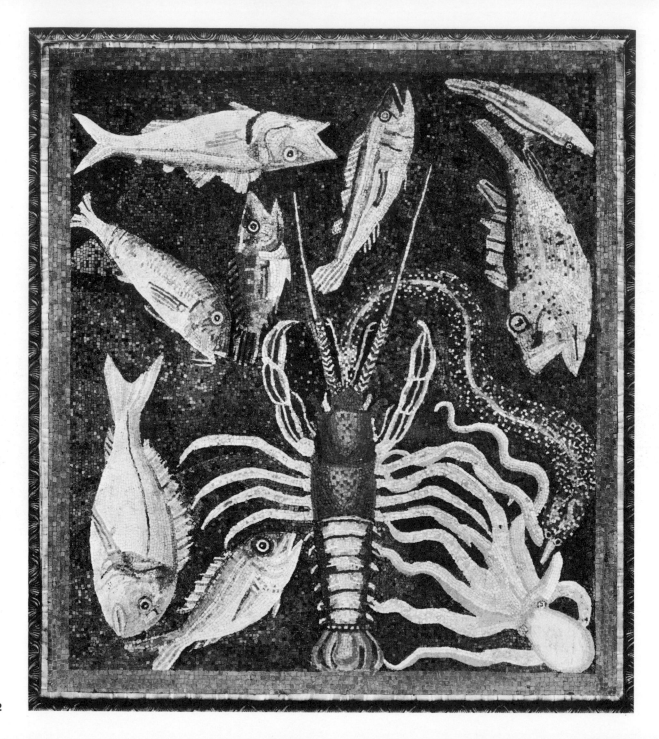

12

AROUND THE FISH by Paul Klee. The undersea motif in this modern painting is treated in a more abstract manner, yet the essential natural forms are evident. (Courtesy: The Museum of Modern Art, Mrs. John D. Rockefeller, Jr., Purchase Fund)

Opposite page:
Roman Mosaic, 2nd century, A.D. Undersea life used in a decorative but realistic manner indicates close study and appreciation of each form. (Courtesy: The Victoria and Albert Museum)

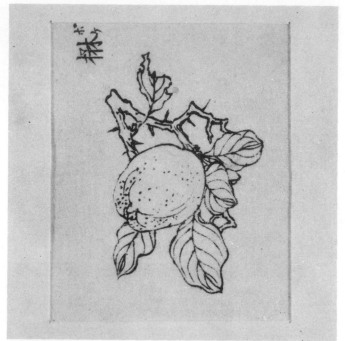

Above left: Kylix, Greece, 5th century, B.C. Decoration in the black-figured style emphasizes the contours of the vessel. The stylized vines and palmetto forms show the artist's interest in nature as source material. (Courtesy: The University Museum, Philadelphia)

Above right: An old Japanese fruit drawing reveals a sensitive understanding of the form. The subtle use of line extends to the calligraphy, itself an art form and an essential part of the design.

Right: One of nature's most perfect spiral designs, this cross section of the nautilus shell reveals its geometric structure. (Photograph: Henry J. Laverty)

Padded Linen Coverlet, Italian, 1400. Variation unified by repeated rectangular shapes. The illustrations tell the story of Tristan. (Courtesy: The Victoria and Albert Museum)

15

Contrast in size and surface gives a variety of textures in this natural random arrangement of rocks and pebbles.

The grain and structure of driftwood form interesting textures, rhythmic lines, and surface patterns. (Photographs: L.B.B.)

Left: Marbelized paper with rhythmic lines formed by chance relates to similar designs found in nature.

Below left: The structure of natural quartz suggests many possibilities for two- or three-dimensional expression. (Photograph: Henry J. Laverty)

Below right: Rhythmic patterns in a formation of micaceus gneiss. (Courtesy: The American Museum of Natural History)

The hexagonal structure of the honeycomb (left) combines a feeling of delicacy with great strength. A direct relationship in architectural structure is seen in a contemporary ceiling (center) in which the designer has used the basic geometric forms to add surface richness to an otherwise bare area. Other examples of hexagonal structure can be seen in the snowflakes (right); each one has almost geometric precision but the fragile beauty of one is never identically repeated in another. (Photographs: left, The American Museum of Natural History; center, John Hoover, Graphic Directions, Inc.)

A ferris wheel with its variety of radiating lines creates its own abstract design. (Photograph: L.B.B.)

Woodpile. (Photograph: L.B.B.)

DANCES AT THE SPRING by Francis Picabia. (Courtesy: Philadelphia Museum of Art, Louise and Walter Arensberg Collection)

The solid forms of the woodpile relate closely to the Picabia
painting, although the painting is deliberately planned to express
movement while the random arrangement of the wood creates a
static design—a beauty all its own.

The symmetrical design and repeated circular elements of an English wrought-iron gate give elegance to the entranceway. (Photograph: L.B.B.)

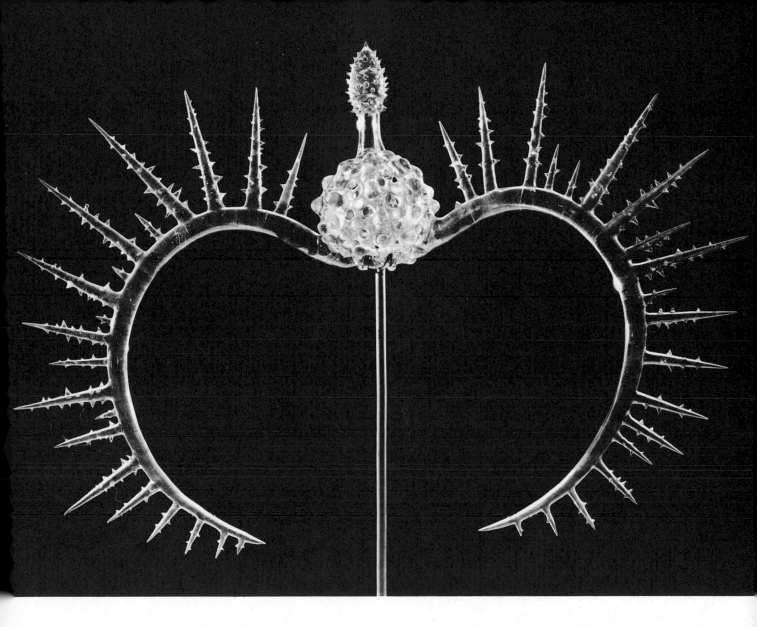

Model gem of Dorcadorpyris dinoceras, an example of nature's order and beauty in a microscopic form. The original from which this model was made is about the size of a grain of sand. Its central balance and circular design seem to relate it to the gate on the opposite page. (Courtesy: The American Museum of Natural History)

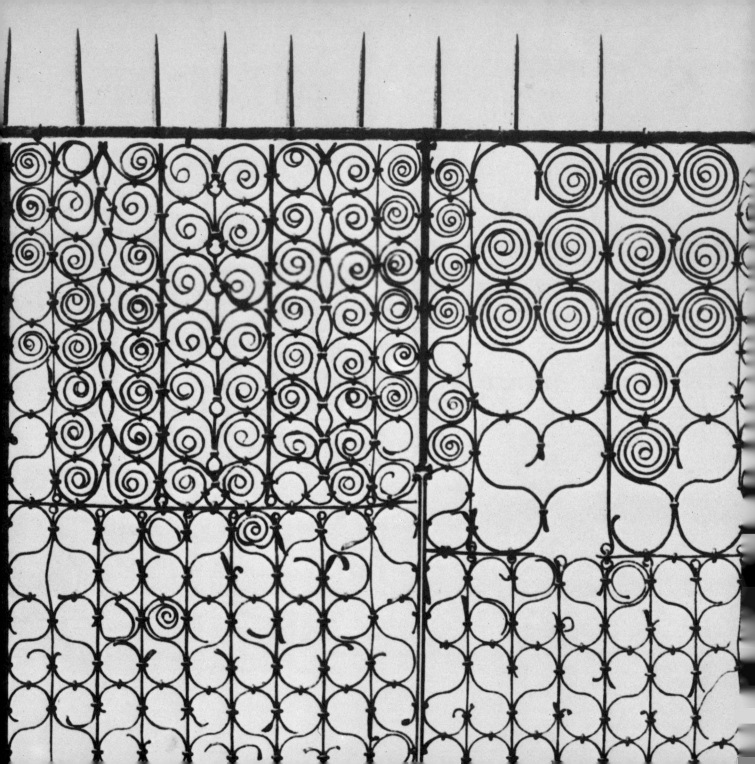

CHAPTER 2 | DESIGN PRINCIPLES

Opposite page:
Wrought Iron Grille, Chichester Cathedral, English, 13th century. Although some details have disappeared, the simple, subtly varied vertical and circular forms that remain give the design a character that is more than geometric. (Courtesy: The Victoria and Albert Museum)

25

The creative urge is a primary force; vision is a basic sensory experience. Both are related to the external world, to the emotions, and to the intellect. But there is a wide chasm between the average individual's ability to think, and his ability to perceive what he sees. Someone once said that few people have mastered their basic ABC's in terms of seeing.

Just as haphazard sounds are not music, nor random words literature, so a mere shape is not art. But uncorrelated sounds, words, or shapes can be the stimulus from which an artistic expression develops. William Harnett, for instance, used the form of a violin in a super-realistic way—almost as a trompe l'oeil, an eye deceiver—to produce, in the 1800's, a composition similar in design to the collages of the twentieth century. And though twentieth century Georges Braque used the same form, along with others, in a still life of abstract shapes, only in its juxtaposition of light and dark areas and the use of similar forms is there a relationship to the Harnett work.

The same familiar shape can stimulate many designers to express many different ideas. For the creative designer continually rediscovers everyday objects, both man-made and natural. He enjoys their touch, their taste, their smell. He "sees" with all his senses, not only with his eyes. Watch a sculptor with a pebble or a shell in his hand. He will hold it, smooth it, turn it over, look at it, and perhaps years later create an abstract form such as the *New Born* by Bran-

cusi. Watch an artist as he walks through the woods. He picks a flower, finds a knarled and twisted root, strokes the bark of the cedar, crushes pine needles for the pungent odor, and many months later may create an abstract or realistic painting with echoes of the forest. Such continual sharpening of the senses leads to greater knowledge and, for the designer, a better understanding of design principles.

The basic elements of the graphic and plastic arts are often considered to be color, line, form, texture, and space. No hard and fast demarcation can be drawn between them. A single design may contain form but line may also be a vital part of the expression. A painting that "sings" of color may use color alone to define form, space, and to suggest texture.

The principles of design—balance, rhythm, emphasis, unity—which are expressed with the elements of color, line, form, texture and space are so interrelated that it is almost impossible to completely isolate them. In discussing one, comments will inevitably be included that could apply equally well to another.

But, first, what do we mean when we say "design"? The word is both a noun and a verb; it has few synonyms but many connotations. As a noun, its connotation was often, and, unfortunately, sometimes still is, something completely separate from the object it enhanced or to which it was "applied." A design was often added on that had no relation to the over-all form or function, sometimes by an artist not even remotely connected with the design of the object itself—antique coffee mills or ceramic cats made into lamps, ashtrays with birds placed on the side that served only to interfere with the placing of pipe or cigarette, streamlined protuberances on furniture and automobiles, in imitation of airplane styling. Even household articles were styled for flight into space. As a reaction against such misuse, emphasis is now placed on the verb "to design," while some artists prefer "order" or "organization" as being more indicative of an action that is an integrated part of the whole. Its emphasis is related to both form and function.

BALANCE implies stability and almost immediately brings to mind the scale or see-saw: identical objects on each side of a centered support, or one or more objects on each side that are different but equal in weight—symmetry and asymmetry.

The predominantly symmetrical, or axial balanced, designs of the Middle Ages may have had a relationship to the great emphasis on religion and the cruciform symbol. At a time of social and psychological turmoil, this relatively static form of balance may have expressed a feeling of sanctuary. Although not used in the early frescoes of Giotto and others, the carved lunettes over the doorways of Gothic churches often showed the figure of Christ with apostles or saints symmetrically balanced on each side.

The Renaissance emphasis on man and humanism resulted in more and more occult or asymmetrical balance. In the Sistine Chapel designs, for instance, the framework of the areas is almost geometrically balanced but the figures within are not. A little later, though not as evident in the other arts, architectural design returned to symmetrical balance as expressed in the Palladian villas. This extended to the eighteenth century churches and colonial homes of America.

More recently, with the emergence of impressionist, expressionist, and abstract schools of art, asymmetrical balance returned as juxtaposition of color and texture as well as form, with occasional apparently random arrangements. By the first half of the twentieth century emphasis often appeared to be on texture alone, as seen in the works of Pollock. Piet Mondrian and other abstract artists achieved a satisfying sense of balance by their placement of similar forms. Examples of balanced design through harmonious arrangement of similar forms and areas of light and dark color can be seen in such essentially different paintings as *Yellow Flowers* by Fernand Leger, *Still Life* by Georges Braque, and *Composition* by Joan Miro.

Artists such as Gris, Klee, and Picasso had an innate sense for balanced arrangement, which might be called optical balance since it cannot be tied too closely to rules. Every competent, sensitive designer develops this sense as his experience grows.

Another form of balance is termed radiation. It is related to symmetrical balance and can be used in two or three dimensions. Contemporary sculptors such as Lippold and Bertoia have expressed this idea in wire and heavy metal. And it may well be one of the oldest expressions of form, it goes back to primitive man's delineation of the sun.

Balance in man-made, three-dimensional structural forms is often achieved by placement of similar or varied geometric shapes. But here also, source material can be found in nature. The domes of Buckminster Fuller seem to have been inspired by the honeycomb structure of the beehive. There is a similarity between suspension bridges and parts of the spider web. The mobiles of Alexander Calder balance in space as do leaf forms on the branch of a tree.

One of nature's most important examples of symmetrical balance is the human figure; among the countless others are butterflies, many trees and flowers. Some trees, particularly those of the fruit varieties, many bushes and vines have asymmetrical balance. Dandelion flowers and seeds, starfish, and anemones are only a few natural radiation forms.

Even the "free forms" so often used in a balanced arrangement in today's design have counterparts in nature. Similarities between these frequently indefinable shapes composed of rhythmic lines encompassing an area or defining a three-dimensional form may be seen in fungi, rocks, microscopic forms, minute sea life, roots, and cloud formations.

Repetition is a basic rhythmic device, as old as art itself. RHYTHM can be produced by continuous repetition, by periodic repetition, or by regular alternation of one or more forms or lines. A single form may be slightly changed with each repetition or be repeated with periodic changes in size. A line may regularly vary in length, weight, or direction. Recurrence of form may be expressed in color or in line.

A wealth of rhythmic repetition can be seen throughout nature and the arts. Continuous repetition of form was used in Stone Age pottery. The egg and dart pattern used in both exterior and interior Greek architectural design is simple alternation. The moldings of Greek, Roman, and Renaissance architecture show alternation of more than two forms. Old nature prints repeat related but different forms. Japanese prints often echo the rhythmic patterns seen in sand.

Another type of rhythmic repetition is called growth or progression. The form grows in size by progressive repetition of its own basic shape. This can be seen in the spiral forms of shells, in fern fronds, in Egyptian palm capitals, and in many Alexander Calder mobiles.

Other rhythmic variations can be seen in all-over patterns as repetition of form in either natural or formal arrangements. Calligraphy expresses rhythm through repetition of both form and line. The all-over patterns in Medieval tapestries often have the natural rhythm seen in a field of daisies or a starry sky. Old

French fabrics and wallpapers were often block printed in all-over formal patterns, while calligraphy and letter forms have been used as design elements in both ancient and modern art and architecture.

Rhythm in art has much the same function as rhythm in music. In music, the ear follows the rhythm of beat and cadence through theme and variations on theme. In art, rhythm leads the eye from one area to another in direct, flowing, or staccato movement. Free brush strokes in a painting can give a swirling sense of motion; an undulating line leads the eye gently from its beginning to its end.

EMPHASIS gives prominence to a particular form or area. A brilliant spot of color dominates a subdued area. Contemporary painters who use abstract and free forms often accent their designs by judicious placement of bright forms or colors against black, subtle grays, or muted colors. Nature exhibits this principle in varied ways: the bright patch of color on a red-winged blackbird, a spot on a butterfly wing, a bright leaf on the brown forest floor.

Emphasis can also be achieved by strength of line, by depth of color, by light, or by greater detail in one area than another. Old manuscripts achieve this by illuminated initial letters or bits of color introduced within the text. One part of a design can be emphasized by contrast in size. Sometimes a different texture or different material can achieve the same result.

When the elements in a design—color, line, form, texture, space—give a satisfying sense of relationship, the design is said to exhibit **UNITY**. Like threads that must be interwoven to make a fabric, the elements must be unified to create a design.

Similar forms, similar lines, related colors, even a backgound color or texture can hold a design together and give a sense of unity. A recurring spot or shape of color can unify the whole. There must, however, be unity with variety otherwise monotony is the result. Sometimes this is achieved by an entirely different shape or spot of color that does not dominate but simply adds variety to an otherwise repetitious design.

The principles of design are guideposts, not answers in themselves. To use them effectively the artist or designer must have an idea to express, a direction or objective in mind. Aesthetic interpretation is vital. Without it, the most conscientious attention to balance, rhythm, emphasis and unity will result in uninteresting work. With it, even though the principles may be forgotten and used only subconsciously, a beautiful design may emerge. The satisfying design is most often the result of both conscious and unconscious effort. Art always starts with an idea.

Irregular free forms of microscopic life bear a striking resemblance to the organic shapes characteristic of Miro.

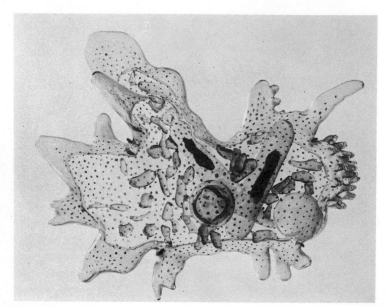

Model of an Amoeba. (Courtesy: The American Museum of Natural History)

COMPOSITION, 1933 by Joan Miro. (Courtesy: Philadelphia Museum of Art, A. E. Gallatin Collection)

A natural iron ore form that is sculptural in quality. Its solid, almost spherical masses seem to relate to the bulk and solidity of the torso.

Hematite from Cumberland, England
(Courtesy: The American Museum of Natural History)

TORSO by Gaston Lachaise. (Courtesy: The Museum of Modern Art, gift of Edward M. M. Warburg)

Ognonet.

(Photograph: Henry J. Laverty)

Wrought Iron, 1876, by Bernard, Bishop, and Barnard, Norwich, England, design by Thomas Jekyll. (Courtesy: The Victoria and Albert Museum)

Two strong symmetrically balanced designs. The natural form of the sunflower has been interpreted to emphasize its basic structure, while the structure of the butterfly is emphasized by repetition of the natural form.

Opposite page:
Fruit Print, French, c. 1700-1800. A strong central design with similar but varied forms gives an unusually pleasant sense of balance.

Above: Chandelier, Mozarabic, c. 700-900 A.D., found in Granada, Spain. A radiating design that uses curved and angular forms and variety in thickness of lines to create a work of art of a functional form. (Courtesy: The Victoria and Albert Museum)

Left: Detail from a Walkway in Cambridge, England. This radiating design of stones turns an ordinary path into a handsome design. (Photograph: Raymond A. Ballinger)

The print (left) is balanced by the flowers that lean to the left of the strong central stem and by the few well placed lines of explanation on the other side. In the page from a Dutch book of the seventeenth century (right) the plant form illustrating the text is a handsome element in an asymmetrical design. A beautiful example of page layout.

LYTHRVM foliis oppofitis cordato lanceolatis, floribus fpicatis dodecandris. *Linn.* S.P. 446. variet. *Salicaria. Ludw.* D.G.P. 734.

Die wurtz nützt man in der ertzney. vñ die ift zu vil fachen gut. Die foll man famlen in dem herbft vñ fy zer fchneiden vñ an ain vaden reichen vñ fy auff hencken vñ die laffen truken werden. geleich den fchwerteln wurtzeln Die wurtz hat grof tuget an jr.als man dañ gefchubñ vindt in dem buch pandecta in dem .criiij. capitel dz fich anhebt puthoimarien ℭ Serapio fpricht. das difer wurtzel tugent fey raingen vñ auffthun die beftopffung. ℭ Dyafcoiides fpricht.das dife wurtzel fey gar gut dem menfchñ genütz mit waffer vñ die getrucken.Vñ fy vertreybt auch feer die gefchwulft des bauchs. vñ benimpt auch dartzu die bofen fleg ma von ain menfchen. dauon fich erhebte die waffer fucht. ℭ Auch alfo getruncke püngt fy den frawñ jr blumen mechtigklich. ℭ Diafcoiides. Wolche fraw uber dife wurtzel gieng fo fy fchwanger war die precht ain tods kind. ℭ Dife wurtz gelegt der frawe an jr huff fo fy geberen fol.fy gebürt zuhandt. ℭ Vo difer wurtz getruncken mit wein trei bet auf vergifft. ℭ Der fafft von difem krautt gelaffen in die nafen. rainiget das haubt. ℭ Sy rainigt auch die muter für all and wurtzel. alfo genützt. ℭ Nym fy vñ fchneyd die klain.gleich würflet vñ thuß in aintuchlein.vñ ainer frawe gehalten in jr fcham fy zeucht vil vnflat an fich.vñ rainigt wol.vñ püngt den frawe jr feuchtigkait.menftruum genant. ℭ wein dariñ gefotten

ift ciclamen.ift gut wiß beftopffug des miltz. ℭ Ciclamen gepuluert. vñ in die wuden d vifteln mit wikñ gelegt.raumbt auf das faul flaifch ℭ Dif puluer in die nafen gethaun beißt auf daz faul flaifch daz dariñ wechft. Dife kranckhait ift genant polipus.

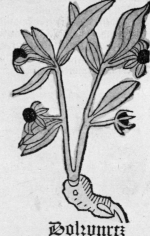

Bolzwurtz
Das ·ccccxix· Capitel
Vua verfa latinect grece.
ℭ Die maifterfprechẽ.daz difes fey ain kraut vnd hab knopff die feind über geftilbt.Dif kraut vñ die wurtzel find kalt vñ feucht am andñ grade. Vñ man braucht in der ertzney. Vnd ift gut genützt für groffe hitz auswendig vñ inwendig des leibs aber fy macht vñ meret die melanco
B ij

Bare branches against the sky create a design reminiscent of calligraphy. (Photograph: Henry W. Ray)

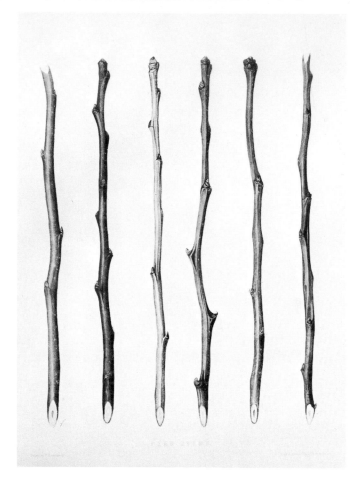

Antique Print

Monreale Cathedral, the Cloister, Sicily, 12th century. (Courtesy: Italian State Tourist Office. Photograph: "ENIT")

Rhythm created by regular alternation. The richly stylized and various surface patterns of the twin columns are emphasized by the plain forms they decorate. Rhythm is seen also in the repetition of pear stems that have sensitively varied forms.

Opposite page:
Well Head from Murano, Italy, c. 900-1000. Unity is achieved by the use of interwoven circular forms, within which are alternating radiating designs. (Courtesy: The Victoria and Albert Museum)

39

CHAPTER 3 | DECORATION A HUMAN NEED

Opposite page:
Mask, Sepik River Area, New Guinea. Decorative lines of reddish paint over white clay empha-size the structure of the face and also relate to the shell form used in the headband. An example of decoration as personal adornment. (Courtesy: The University Museum, Philadelphia)

41

Decoration has been a part of life ever since Paleolithic man first painted his caves. Since then decoration, as have all the arts, has continued to be related to man's religious ceremonies and beliefs. It has also been used as a means of communication—for teaching, honoring and identifying—as bodily ornamentation, as ornamentation of utilitarian objects, and sometimes as decoration for the sake of decoration alone.

The carved standards, masks, beads and woven materials of primitive peoples are examples of decoration done without conscious concepts of art, yet with purpose and a sense of fitness for the material used.

The inscribed Mayan or Aztec stellae was a calendar in stone. The totem poles of the Northwest Indians recorded the history of family or tribe. Early frescoes and mosaics, the carvings and stained glass windows of Medieval churches were instructional "visual aids" as well as acts of artistic and religious devotion.

Palace gates of intricately designed wrought iron, heraldic symbols on flags, standards, and shields identified members of the nobility and their followers and showed their rank. Coronation designs, etched glass goblets, silver bowls, glassware and fabrics often recorded an event or honored an individual. Carved and painted shop signs identified the product to be sold.

Man has long used decorative design to enhance his utilitarian objects. Stone Age man decorated his pottery, using his innate urge to beautify to emphasize form. Early Greek and many European coins were unusually well-designed, though the designs added nothing to their monetary value. And Medieval tapestries, used primarily to shut out the cold of stone walls, also added the warmth of their rich designs. Lovingly designed patchwork quilts gave beauty to the early American home. Even games have been elaborately designed when plain forms would have sufficed.

But in the twentieth century, decoration became an almost "naughty" word, rejected as was the word "pattern." This is especially apparent when we look at the stark simplicity of twentieth century design in architecture. Nevertheless, man's urge to enrich his surroundings continued. Today it may be expressed in a different way. Perhaps the billboards, the neon lights, the covers of paperback books, the increasing use of ceramic tile or mosaic murals, even the excessive interest in makeup and fashion relate to that basic urge.

In contrast to our uncluttered rooms and the geometric forms of our skyscrapers, the past as a whole seems to show greater emphasis on decoration. But the past is so overgrown with sentiment that it is difficult to study in terms of understanding and evaluation. Motives, as well as examples, are endless but often obscured by the passage of time. We do know that decoration ebbs and flows in an almost predictable rhythm. Along with the other arts, it mirrors, and sometimes forecasts, changing times.

The high tide of the Renaissance period flowed into the Baroque and Rococo and these into imitative classicism. The swing from the extremes of Baroque and Rococo decoration to the relative simplicity of the Classic revival is roughly paralleled by extremes in human thought. The rich pagaentry of Queen Elizabeth's England ebbed into the austerity of the Commonwealth and the spread of Puritan influence; the eighteenth century lavishness of Louis XV and XVI led to the French revolution.

The impact of the machine era brought late nineteenth century pseudo-Gothic and sentimental Victorian design into disfavor. Shortly after that, streamlining was carried to ridiculous extremes. In the twentieth century the forces behind design, and the results they produce, seemed to be better understood. A greater interest developed in the relationship of material to function. Decorative design began to be thought of as an organic part of a whole rather than as an isolated afterthought.

All the arts do not always march together in reflecting the times. It is, for instance, interesting to note a contrasting emphasis on design that occurred simultaneously with the trend toward architectural simplicity. Such painters as Henri Matisse, Fernand Léger, Jean Lurçat, Marc Chagall, and Joan Miro also applied their skills and ideas to tapestries, pottery, and religious art and architecture. Decoration in its best sense was given a new impetus.

To live in a completely stark and bare world would soon drive man to decorate. And history would repeat itself. Half-hearted copying, conscious application without understanding would again result only in the insignificance of mediocre design, while design that expressed vigor, spirit, and sincerity of purpose would survive.

Left: Reminiscent of 18th century glass, the design of this goblet commemorating the coronation of Elizabeth II melds form and decoration with a dignity suitable to the occasion. (Photograph: Henry J. Laverty)

Opposite page:
Stone Capital, Auvergne, France, 1st quarter of the 12th century. Carved angels holding sentences from the Gospels taught the faithful and also enriched the interior of the church. (Courtesy: The Victoria and Albert Museum)

Veneered Backgammon Board. The carved details and geometric marquetry with various wood veneers relate to the quality of precision that is an important part of the game. (Courtesy: The Victoria and Albert Museum)

Opposite page:
The Lord's Prayer, cut by T. Hunter, 1786. A formal arrangement of cut paper designed with skill and reverence. Contrasting curved and straight lines provide a delicate frame for the text in the central form. (Courtesy: The Victoria and Albert Museum)

Hawk, Egyptian Faience, late dynastic period, 500-550 B.C. (Courtesy: The Metropolitan Museum of Art, Carnarvon Collection, gift of Edward S. Harkness)

The decorative use of inlay to delineate the hawk's feathers relates them in a semi-realistic way to their structure in nature. In contrast, a more whimsical use of design makes the hippopotamus seem to stand amidst the lotus blossoms that decorate him.

Hippopotamus from Tomb of Senbi, Meir, 12th Dynasty, Egypt. (Courtesy: The Metropolitan Museum of Art, gift of Edward S. Harkness, 1926)

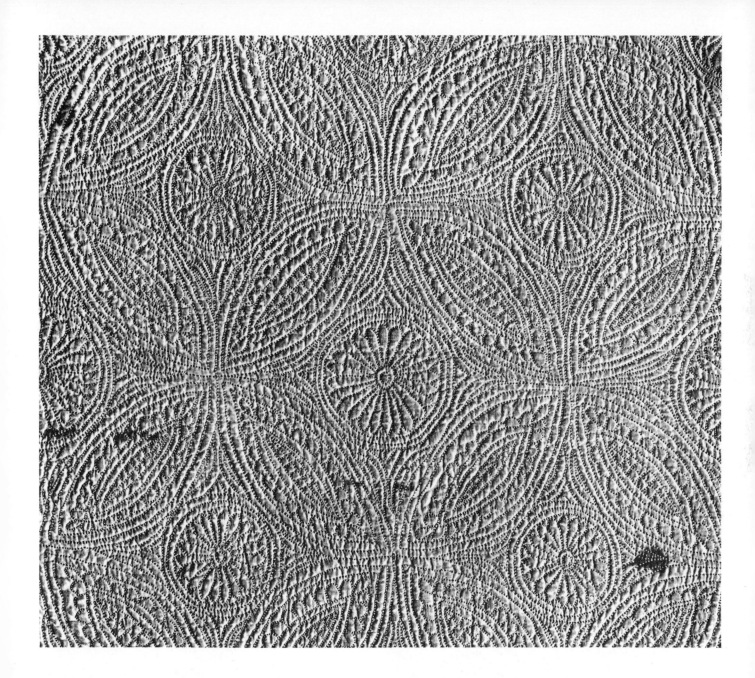

Linen Quilted Coverlet, English, 1st half of the 18th century. Interwoven circular and radiating forms produce a rich textural surface and a satisfying over-all design. (Courtesy: The Victoria and Albert Museum)

Below left: Chancel Ceiling, Tewksbury Abbey, England. This unusual example of interweaving radiating lines held together by circular forms commemorates the Yorkist victory over the Lancastrians in 1471. The "Stellas" in the center boss represent the "Suns of Splendor of the House of York." (Photograph: Courtesy of F. Frith & Co., Ltd.)

Below right: Spanish Wrought Iron Standard, early 16th century. The choice of symbolic forms used in this symmetrically balanced design indicates an emblem of authority. (Courtesy: The Victoria and Albert Museum)

Bands of contrasting colors strengthen the centralized architectural design of a chemist's shop in England. The lettering is beautifully integrated into the design. (Photograph: L.B.B.)

TAPESTRY VERDURE, detail from Arras, France, c. 1300-1400. Variety in the forms and their placement and loving attention to details of nature give a satisfying rhythm to this design without

detracting from the story it tells. No two nature forms or details are identical. (Courtesy: The Victoria and Albert Museum)

Lady Mary Mosaic Floor, from the Early Christian Church at Beth Shan, Israel. Religious text and geometric forms are combined on this example of floor decoration. Slight variations in the sprightly birds enliven the strong unity of the interlocking circles. (Courtesy: The University Museum, Philadelphia)

Opposite page:

Above left: Medusa Mask, Roman Bath Museum, Bath, England. An age-old symbol. The radiating forms emphasize the features and create a strongly unified design. (Photograph: courtesy of the City of Bath Corp.)

Above right: White Earthenware Bowl, Kashan, Persia, early 13th century. A rhythmic arrangement of stylized leaves and vines. The circular movement relates to the form. (Courtesy: The Victoria and Albert Museum)

Below: Ionic Capital, Greece, IV century, B.C. The spiral forms and the egg and dart moulding became an example of classic design that influenced architects and designers for many centuries. (Courtesy: The Metropolitan Museum of Art, gift of the American Society for the Excavation of Sardis, 1926)

Opposite page:
The basic egg shape offers a wide variety of opportunities for effective repetition and alternation of geometric, natural, and symbolic forms. (Arrangement and designs by Arthur P. Williams. Photograph: Tony Calabro)

Inca Pottery Vessel. Repetition of age-old geometric patterns emphasizes the vessel's basic form. A highly effective example of decoration for an object of everyday use. (Courtesy: The University Museum, Philadelphia)

Dandelions gone to seed in the field. One of nature's many random designs. (Photograph: Henry W. Ray)

A typical old French woodblock. Repeated printing of the block produced an all over design on fabrics. (Photograph: Henry J. Laverty)

Opposite page:
MERRY JESTERS by Henri Rousseau. Decorative, boldly painted plants provide a rich foil for the mysterious animal forms cowering in the center. (Courtesy: The Philadelphia Museum of Art, Louise and Walter Arensberg Collection)

Left: Prestige Money, Northwest Indian, U.S.A. Similar in general form to the column, but much more stylized, the copper piece known as Tina, prestige money, uses thick and thin lines in a balanced masklike design that relates to the shape of the piece. (Courtesy: The University Museum, Philadelphia). *Right:* Walnut Column, Salerno, Italy, late 12th century. Carv- ing on the column includes a figure of the prophet Jeremiah and allegorical figures as well as an imaginative use of styl- ized natural forms. The vertical figures and vines repeat the upward movement of the column while the band of repeated leaf forms emphasizes the structural change in its width. (Courtesy: The Victoria and Albert Museum)

Opposite page:
Above: The gate shadow on the wall in France shows a combination of oval and circular forms. Rhythmic shapes reinforced by the structure of the gate give a solid yet deco- rative design. (Photograph: L.B.B.). *Below:* Copper Cookie Molds, Swedish, early 19th century. The urge to decorate has always applied to food. Designs are still used when a plain circular form would do just as well. (Photograph: Henry J. Laverty)

Santa Maria del Fiore, Florence, 14th century. Various kinds of colored marble are arranged in geometric, structural designs that emphasize the vertical and circular basic forms. (Photo: L.B.B.)

Mosaics, San Marco, Venice, 11th century. A rich mosaic, blending vertical and domed forms, re-creates the ornate façade of the Cathedral of San Marco. This representation, with its multitude of human figures at the base, beautifully fits the space for which it was designed. (Photograph: L.B.B.)

Ca' d'Oro, Venice, 1st half of the 15th century. Decorative structural forms lend an airy elegance to the façade of this late Gothic building. (Photograph: L.B.B.)

CHAPTER 4 | DESIGN TODAY

Opposite page:
HOMAGE TO THE SQUARE: SILENT HALL by Joseph Albers. This is one of many similar paint-ings based on the rectangle or square that demonstrate the relativity of color and interacting simple components. The square as a basic element of design is comparatively scarce in nature. (Courtesy: The Museum of Modern Art, Dr. and Mrs. Frank Stanton Fund)

The cultural pattern of any era is revealed by the work of its artists, craftsmen, and designers. Medieval art speaks of scholasticism and religion; the art of the Renaissance of enlightened, active searching.

Today's designer views his rich inheritance from the past with an inquiring mind, seeking to understand the forces that molded the thought, and therefore the products, of each age. His many streams of influence run from ancient cultures through the arts and "isms" that span the later eighteen and early nineteen hundreds.

In the late nineteenth century, when architecture was struggling to follow painting in freeing itself from classical imitation, and decorative design was still influenced by Victorian lavishness, mechanization made itself felt. The machine replaced the craftsman. Objects, fabrics, furniture and buildings were mass produced for mass purchase. Quantity superceded quality. As a result many objects were badly designed, shoddy, or just cheap imitations.

Although there was revolt against the machine age —the rebellion of Futurism, Cubism and Expressionism was a turning inwards expressed in tensions of color and form—there was no constructive effort to adjust to it until 1919 when the Bauhaus was established in Weimar, Germany. This new impetus to the arts was founded by the young architect Walter Gropius; its purpose, to fuse the aesthetics of the visual arts with the needs of mass production by combining the skills of artist and artisan. The school existed for only 14 years but when it was closed in 1933 by the National Socialists, the dispersal of its staff and students scattered its spirit to many lands. It is still considered one of the most important and vital influences on the arts of the twentieth century.

The possibility of turning out standardized products that were well designed came to be accepted. Even though the subtle irregularities of the handmade objects were eliminated, products of the machine came to be seen in a new light. Greater interest in the function of objects made designers more conscious of three-dimensional form, so form became important and the possibilities inherent in planes and surfaces were carefully explored. There was greater awareness of texture in materials and greater interest in the honest use of materials as media. Balance, especially asymmetric balance, was studied and geometric parts became important facets of the whole. Emphasis was on form and function while simplicity became a refreshing change from mere surface decoration—until simplicity itself went to extremes.

Scandinavian design, indirectly influenced by the Bauhaus, has had a quality unique unto itself, a warmth that sets it apart. Its glassware, rugs, jewelry, furniture and architecture have, for the most part, a rich simplicity that takes into account the essential quality of the material and process used. Wood surfaces are often merely oiled and polished to enhance the grain of the wood; glass is neither "tortured" nor over-etched. The inherent quality and color of the glass predominates. This approach is apparent in most Scandinavian designs and has had an influence on designers in many parts of the world.

Painting, sculpture, fabrics, and the graphic arts all felt the pervasive effect of modern architecture. Its squares, cubes, spheres, triangles, and cylinders are still a part of living today; they surround us in both public and private buildings. It was almost predictable that emphasis upon geometric forms would create a new interest in the highly organized, structurally planned forms of nature.

Designers began to see relationships in natural

forms that relieved the almost sterile austerity of the reactionary period. They became aware that natural forms, whether seen with the naked eye or through the microscope, also had relationships between form and function. Natural forms became subjects of study, not in order to copy or interpret their outward shapes but to absorb and use their principles of structure. Nature's many examples of free forms—rhythmic lines enclosing form or space—were used by artists, sculptors and architects to express ideas, and then often translated for use in fabrics, jewelry, ceramics, and household articles. There seemed to be a general return to, a reaffirmation of, the basic elements of creative expression: color, form, line, texture, and space.

In spite of the fresh wind of change blown by the Bauhaus and the influences which followed, the market was and still is being flooded with cheap, badly designed articles of every nature. The non-selective individual is surrounded with an overwhelming amount of inferior examples of furniture, automobiles, household objects, and fabrics. But progress is being made. More well-designed examples are appearing. Exhibits of good design by museums and design groups have helped.

And most recently, the arts have felt the impact of science. New worlds of color, line, and form are now part of the expanding visible world. Today's designer is becoming more and more aware of this new source material from nature. Abstractions derived from forms revealed by science have been used in corporation advertising and in industrial design. As science continues to probe into the unknown, the artist will share the excitement of new discoveries; new forms and concepts to be used with imagination and integrity as a reflection of the expanding world he lives in.

Along with a forward looking attitude, there is also a growing appreciation of the past. No longer are interiors cold and sterile "modern." They are simple, perhaps, and uncluttered, but often enhanced by a strong primitive piece or a subtle example of Chinese porcelain. The designer has taken off his blinders and looks in many directions. He sees a Persian rug or a piece of Medieval sculpture not merely as historical objects but as design forms that contrast well with his bare walls and undecorated furniture. He knows that design is still related to living in the contemporary world, that form, function, and material still work together. But rules that were rigidly applied a few decades ago, in a period of transition, though still understood and respected, are not now rigidly adhered to. Individual expression has again become an essential part of the aesthetics of design.

Awareness of nature, appreciation of the past, and scientific knowledge equip today's designer, artist, and craftsman to collaborate with those who produce. Perhaps a new Renaissance will emerge so that from our civilization arts will develop that not only reflect the spirit of the age but once more those timeless qualities inherent in the good design of any era.

Model of Lithocircus Magnificus. One of the most remarkable of the Radiolaria, this minute marine form bears a resemblance to some contemporary metal and wire sculptures. A combination of solid and airy forms, it is an excellent example of balanced radiating design. (Courtesy: The American Museum of Natural History)

THE SUN by Richard Lippold. An example of radiation that uses line only to define form and space. Made of gold-filled wire, this unique and seemingly fragile design has great strength and size. (Courtesy: The Metropolitan Museum of Art, Fletcher Fund, 1956)

Sterling Silver Necklace by Louise B. Ballinger. Similar abstract forms repeated in varying sizes express the design principle of growth. (Photograph: Henry J. Laverty)

A simple geometric shape designed for a purpose. The radiating folds on the top are an interesting contrast to the simple cylindrical form of the container. (Courtesy: The Museum of Modern Art)

Advertisement for Olivetti Underwood Corporation. A balanced arrangement of simple abstract shapes derived from obvious forms, combined with the well-placed name, suggest the idea of communication with a portable typewriter.

Scandinavian Glass. Contemporary glass exhibits a sensitive awareness of the quality and color of the glass itself. It needs no embellishment. (Photograph: Henry J. Laverty)

SANCTUARY by Seymour Lipton. A sculptural arrangement of overlapping circular pieces that relates closely to natural forms. (Courtesy: The Museum of Modern Art, Blanchette Rockefeller Fund)

SEED POD by Donald Irving. The texture and rhythm of these angular and radiating metal shapes express the bursting seed pod.

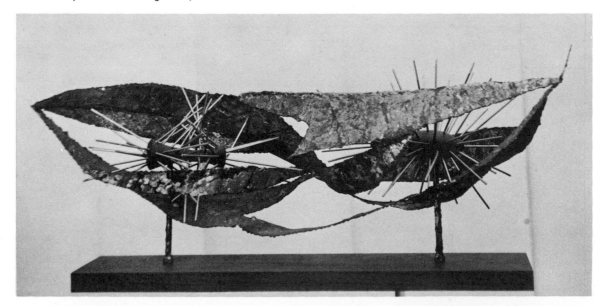

BIG BOY by Isamu Noguchi. Although there is an implication of a complete human form, the emphasis is on the contrasting abstract shapes and plastic quality of the material. (Courtesy: The Museum of Modern Art, A. Conger Goodyear Fund)

Eero Saarinen's dramatic headquarters building for the Columbia Broadcasting System as it nears completion and (left) showing various aspects of its construction. The contrast of density and texture in the alternating vertical bands of granite and glass creates a feeling of classical elegance and plasticity rare in modern skyscraper architecture. (Photographs: courtesy the Columbia Broadcasting System)

Scandinavian Teakwood Bowl, designed by Paul E. Killinger. The simplicity of this piece shows an excellent regard for the material and emphasizes the texture and grain of the wood. (Courtesy: The American Craftsmen's Council)

Opposite page:
SKY CATHEDRAL by Louise Nevelson. Solid geometric and irregular forms arranged within rectangular boxes using imagination and ingenuity create a wall panel that emphasizes the solidity and textural variety of the wood. (Courtesy: The Museum of Modern Art, gift of Mr. and Mrs. Ben Mildwoff)

Rhythmic free forms bear a relationship that gives unity to the work and also seem related to natural organic forms.

CONFIGURATION by Jean Arp.
(Courtesy: The Philadelphia Museum of Art, A. E. Gallatin Collection)

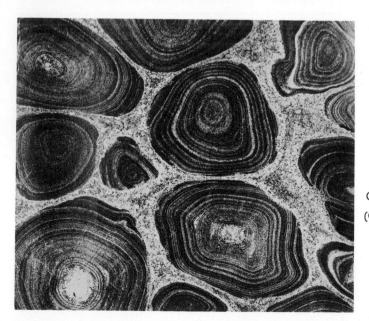

Orbicular Granite, Finland.
(Courtesy: The American Museum of Natural History)

The similar forms and use of line seen in the woven piece and the wire basket are put to entirely different purposes.

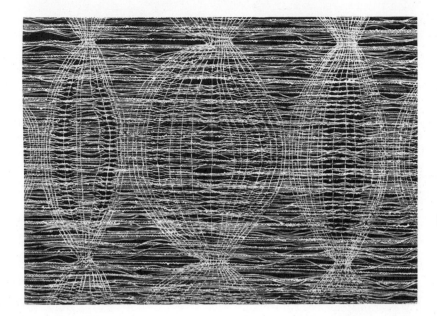

Woven Space Divider by Pamela Stearns.
(Courtesy: The American Craftsmen's Council)

Salad Basket by M. Schimmel.
(Courtesy: The Museum of Modern Art)

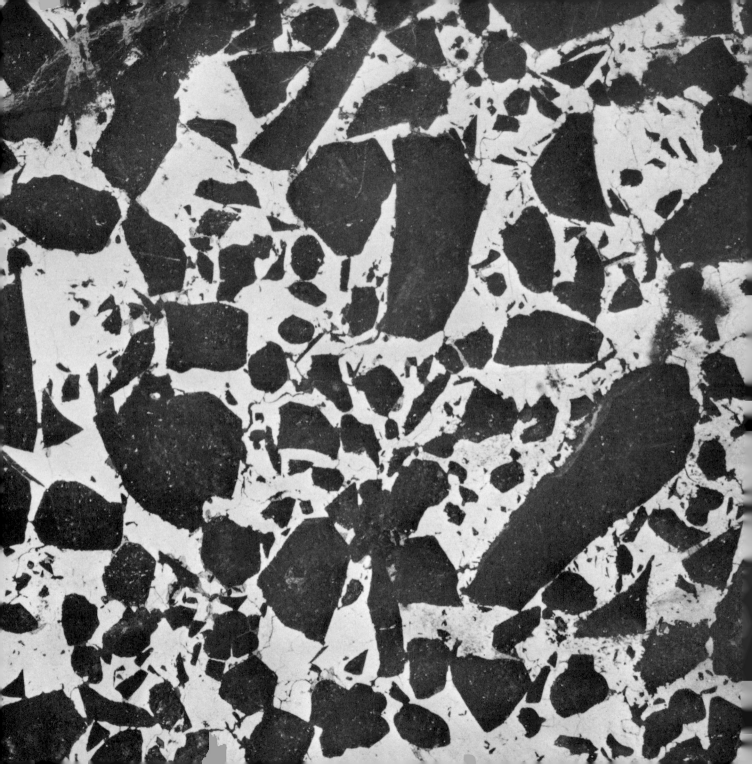

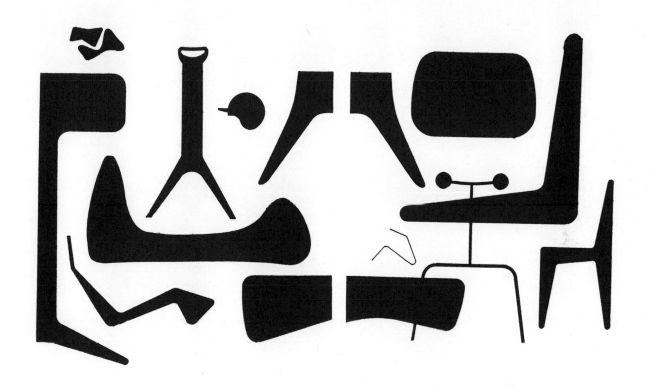

Chart of Furniture Forms for Irving Associates, designed by George Nelson. An abstract composition based on contemporary functional shapes. (Courtesy: The Museum of Modern Art)

Opposite page:
Meteorite, Australia. Such natural shapes often serve as source material for contemporary designs and paintings. (Courtesy: The American Museum of Natural History)

ARTIST: ARTHUR WILLIAMS

ADAM SMITH

on the source of wealth

It is the great

multiplication of the

productions of

all the different arts,

in consequence of

the division of labour,

which occasions, in

a well-governed society,

that universal

opulence which extends

itself to the lowest

ranks of the people.

(*Wealth of Nations, 1776*)

CONTAINER CORPORATION OF AMERICA

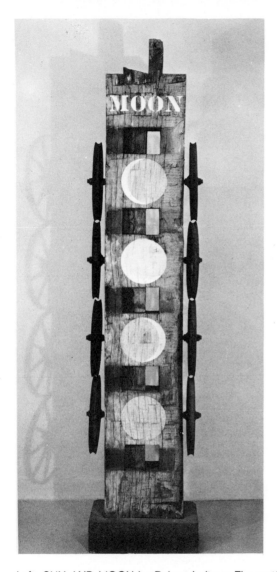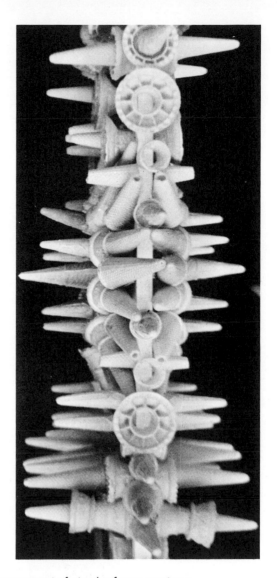

Left: SUN AND MOON by Robert Indiana. The vertical arrangement of circular forms creates a whimsical example of Pop Art. (Courtesy: The Museum of Modern Art, Philip C. Johnson Fund)

Right: Ice cream cones create an appropriate, eye-catching window display. (Photograph: L.B.B.)

Opposite page:
An inventive use of basic three-dimensional forms to express an idea. The vertical arrangement repeated in the type results in a well designed layout. (Courtesy: The Container Corporation of America. Artist, Arthur P. Williams; Art Director, Walter Reinsel)

84

CHIEF by Franz Kline. Bold brush lines express the power of authority. (Courtesy: The Museum of Modern Art, gift of Mr. and Mrs. David M. Salinger)

Opposite page:
CHARLES BAUDELAIRE by Henri Matisse. In any art expression the quality of line relates to the form and the idea. Delicate but sure lines suggest the subject's strong, sensitive nature. (Courtesy: The Museum of Modern Art, Abby Aldrich Rockefeller Fund)

PAINTING by Jackson Pollack. This seemingly random arrangement of irregular lines results in a bold textural quality and an active surface pattern characteristic of much contemporary art. (Courtesy: The Museum of Modern Art, Gift of Mr. and Mrs. Ira Haupt)

Opposite page:
JAMES MADISON by Thomas F. Vroman. In the advertisement, line is used in a decorative manner to enrich and strengthen the different color areas and to emphasize the form that expresses an abstract idea. (Courtesy: The Container Corporation of America)

Artist: Thomas Vroman

James Madison
ON THE DANGERS TO LIBERTY

I believe there are more instances of the abridgment of the
freedom of the people by gradual and silent encroachments
of those in power than by violent and sudden usurpations.

Speech in the Virginia Convention, June 16, 1788

CONTAINER CORPORATION OF AMERICA

Left: LUCKY STRIKE by Stuart Davis. Contemporary forms and bold colors are characteristic of the work of this artist—an advertisement definitely of the twentieth century. (Courtesy: The Museum of Modern Art, gift of the American Tobacco Company, Inc.)

Right: PARALLEL FORMS II by A. E. Gallatin. A painting using variations on the basic rectangular form with a designer's regard for the dynamic potential of negative space. (Courtesy: The Metropolitan Museum of Art, gift of R. Thornton Wilson, 1952)

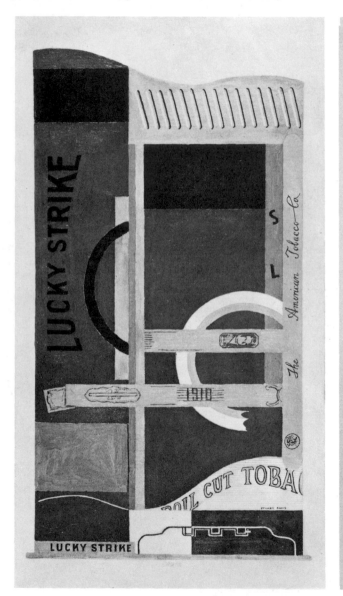

Packages, designed by Raymond A. Ballinger. An irregular radiating form in several colors suggests a "gay mood." The same form is adapted to the various sizes and proportions of the perfume containers. (Courtesy: Frances Denney, Inc.)

FAMILY GROUP by Henry Moore. Positive and negative space is organized and a rhythmic flow of form seen with directness and simplicity in this expression of the human figure. (Courtesy: The Museum of Modern Art, A. Conger Goodyear Fund)

Asphalt Paving. The flow of lines created by asphalt has a curious resemblance to many contemporary paintings. (Photograph: Henry W. Ray)

BIRD IN SPACE by Constantin Brancusi. This sculpture has a timeless quality, a nature symbol of great simplicity. (Courtesy: The Philadelphia Museum of Art, Louise and Walter Arensberg Collection)

OPPOSITION OF LINES: RED AND YELLOW by Piet Mondrian. The rigid balancing of horizontal and vertical lines and rectangles of color expresses the preoccupation with geometric forms in the twentieth century. (Courtesy: The Philadelphia Museum of Art, A. E. Gallatin Collection)

Section of Geodesic Dome, designed by Buckminster Fuller. This type of construction is evidence of the principles of structure found in nature. (Photograph: Alex Georges)

CASTELLON DE LA PLANA by Sylvia Steiner. The batik design shows evidence of the source material in its geometric forms and strong architectural feeling. (Courtesy: The American Craftsmen's Council)

Left: CONSTELLATION WITH RED OBJECT by Alexander Calder. Related shapes create an abstract design that suggests life and movement. (Courtesy: The Museum of Modern Art, James Thrall Soby Fund)

Below: GIANT MOLECULES, drawing by Eric Mose. An interesting design composed of symbols of molecules. (From the artist's portfolio Art in Science, II. Copyright 1957 by Scientific American, Inc. All rights reserved)

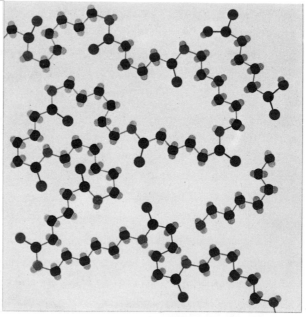

BIBLIOGRAPHY

Bazin, Germain. *A History of Art*. New York: Bonanza Books, 1959.

Bevlin, Marjorie Elliott. *Design Through Discovery*. New York: Holt, Rinehart and Winston, 1963.

Borten, Helen. *Do You See What I See?* London and New York: Abelard and Schuman, 1959.

Canaday, John. *Mainstreams of Modern Art*. New York: Simon and Schuster, 1962.

Collier, Graham. *Form, Space and Vision*. Englewood Cliffs, New Jersey: Prentice-Hall, Inc., 1962.

Downer, Marion. *Discovering Design*. New York: Lothrop, Lee and Shepard Company, Inc., 1947.

Edman, Irwin. *Arts and the Man*. New York: W. W. Norton and Company, Inc., 1939.

Emerson, Sybil. *Design a Creative Approach*. Scranton, Pennsylvania: International Textbook Company.

Ghiselin, Brewster. *The Creative Process*. Berkeley, California: University of California Press, 1952.

Goldwater, Robert. *Modern Art in Your Life*. New York: Museum of Modern Art.

Kainz, Louise and Riley, Olive. *Exploring Art*. New York: Harcourt, Brace and Company, 1951.

Kepes, Gyorgy. *Language of Vision*. Chicago: Paul Theobald, 1944.

Krutch, Joseph Wood. *Experience of Art*. New York: Collier Books, 1962.

Larkin, Oliver. *Art and Life in America*. New York: Holt, Rinehart and Winston, 1960. (Revised Edition.)

Lichten, Frances. *Folk Art of Rural Pennsylvania*. New York: Charles Scribner, 1946.

Lipman, Jean. *American Folk Art*. New York: Pantheon Books, Inc.

Manley, Seon. *Adventures in Making*. New York: Vanguard Press, 1959.

Moholy-Nagy, Lazlo. *The New Vision*. New York: Wittenborn, Inc., 1947.

Moseley, Spencer; Johnson, Pauline; and Koenig, Hazel. *Crafts Design*. Belmont, California: Wadsworth Publishing Company, 1962.

Ozenfant, Amadee. *Foundations of Modern Art*. New York: Dover Publications, 1952.

Riley, Olive. *Your Art Heritage*. New York: Harper and Brothers, 1952.

Santayana, George. *The Sense of Beauty*. New York: Dover Publications, 1955.

Scott, Robert Gillam. *Design Fundamentals*. New York: McGraw-Hill Book Company, Inc., 1951.

Strache, Wolf. *Forms and Patterns in Nature*. New York: Pantheon Books, Inc., 1956.

Taylor, Francis Henry. *Fifty Centuries of Art*. New York: Harper and Brothers, 1954.

Taylor, Harold. *Art and the Intellect*. New York: Museum of Modern Art, 1960.

Any publication small or large is the result of the efforts of more than a few minds and hands and this one is no exception. We wish to acknowledge with appreciation all the assistance given us to obtain the variety of material presented here. Museums, libraries, organizations, and individuals both here and abroad have been most gracious in consenting to the use of their material and those immediately concerned have been extremely helpful.

We wish especially to acknowledge the assistance and encouragement of our editor, Sterling McIlhany of Reinhold Publishing Corporation. His interest, his response to our ideas, and his cooperation have made this book a reality.

To Thelma Vroman and Raymond A. Ballinger we gratefully acknowledge continued interest, helpful criticism and encouragement as well as inspiration for this project.

L.B.B.
T.V.

"One can never experience art through descriptions. Explanations and analyses can serve at best as intellectual preparation. They may, however, encourage one to make a direct contact with works of art."

From the New Vision and Abstract of an Artist
by Lazlo Moholy-Nagy
George Wittenborn Inc.
1018 Madison Avenue, New York.